W9-CPF-018

THE CIVIL RIGHTS MOVEMENT

COME.... TOGETHER
Let Us Build A
Non-Violent World

DRAMA OF AFRICAN-AMERICAN HISTORY

THE CIVIL RIGHTS MOVEMENT

by IRMA McCLAURIN
with VIRGINIA SCHOMP

 Marshall Cavendish
Benchmark
New York

ACKNOWLEDGMENTS

With thanks to Jill Watts, professor of history at California State University, San Marcos, for her perceptive comments on the manuscript, and to the late Richard Newman, civil rights advocate, author, and senior research officer at the W. E. B. DuBois Institute at Harvard University, for his excellent work in formulating the series.

DEDICATION

To my nieces and nephew, Justin Thomas and Sydney Rose Wright and Jordan Grace and Angela Renee McClaurin, the youth who will inherit tomorrow, and to the memory of James Haskins, my mentor, who began writing it all. I am grateful to Denzil McKenzie for pushing me and providing me with unwavering encouragement and support.

EDITOR: JOYCE STANTON   PUBLISHER: MICHELLE BISSON
ART DIRECTOR: ANAHID HAMPARIAN   SERIES DESIGNER: MICHAEL NELSON

MARSHALL CAVENDISH BENCHMARK 99 WHITE PLAINS ROAD TARRYTOWN, NEW YORK 10591-9001 www.marshallcavendish.us Text copyright © 2008 Irma McClaurin All rights reserved. No part of this book may be reproduced or utilized in any form or by any means electronic or mechanical including photocopying, recording, or by any information storage and retrieval system, without permission from the copyright holders. All Internet sites were available and accurate when this book was sent to press. LIBRARY OF CONGRESS CATALOGING-IN-PUBLICATION DATA: McClaurin, Irma. The Civil Rights Movement / by Irma McClaurin, with Virginia Schomp. p. cm. — (Drama of African-American history) Summary: "Covers the struggle of African Americans to gain their civil rights, from Brown v. Board of Education in 1954 through the turbulent Sixties"—Provided by publisher. Includes bibliographical references and index. ISBN 978-0-7614-2642-4 1. Civil rights movements—United States—History—20th century—Juvenile literature. 2. African Americans—Civil rights—History—Juvenile literature. I. Schomp, Virginia. II. Title. III. Series. E185.61.M476 2008 323.0973—dc22 2007034729

Images provided by Debbie Needleman, Picture Researcher, Portsmouth, NH, from the following sources: Cover: Bettmann/CORBIS; Back cover: Time Life Pictures/Getty Images; Page i: Inalienable, 2001 (oil on canvas) by Colin Bootman (Contemporary Artist). ©Private Collection/ The Bridgeman Art Library; pages ii-iii, 38, 45: Danny Lyon/Magnum Photos; pages vi, 27, 62: Flip Schulke/CORBIS; pages viii, 13, 15, 41, 50: Time Life Pictures/Getty Images; page ix: Courtesy Chicago Defender; pages 10, 18, 29, 46, 48, 58, 66 top, 69: Associated Press; page 16: Bob Fitch/Black Star; pages 20, 21, 22, 26, 30, 31, 36, 39, 40, 42, 59, 61, 65, 67, 73: Bettmann/CORBIS; pages 24, 25: Courtesy of Mississippi Department of Archives & History; page 32: Jack Moebes/CORBIS; page 35: Eve Arnold/Magnum Photos; page 44: Bob Adelman/Magnum Photos; page 51: Ivan Massar/Black Star; pages 52, 57, 66 bottom: "1976 Matt Herron/Take Stock; page 54: Steve Schapiro/CORBIS; page 64: Copyright 1965 – The Spider Martin Civil Rights Collection – All Rights Reserved – Used With Permission; page 71: Ted Streshinsky/CORBIS

Printed in China
1 3 5 6 4 2

A NOTE ON LANGUAGE

The quoted material appearing in this book includes outdated words such as "colored" and "Negro," which were commonly used by both black and white Americans until the late twentieth century.

Front cover: Fifteen-year-old Elizabeth Eckford was one of the first black students at Central High School in Little Rock, Arkansas.
Back cover: Churchgoers pray for the safety of civil rights activists in 1961.
Half-title page: Martin Luther King Jr.
Title page: Robert Moses *(right)* and a fellow civil rights worker in Greenwood, Mississippi.

CONTENTS

INTRODUCTION

The Civil Rights Movement is the ninth volume in the series Drama of African-American History. Earlier books in this series have followed the journey of black Americans from the start of the transatlantic slave trade in the fifteenth century all the way to the end of World War II in the mid-twentieth century. Now we turn to one of the most exciting chapters in African-American history, the civil rights movement of the 1950s and 1960s.

The struggle against racial discrimination did not start or end with the civil rights movement. In fact, African Americans had begun their freedom fight centuries earlier. Hundreds of slave mutinies took place aboard the ships that transported captive Africans to the Americas. From colonial times through the Civil War, black men and women protested their enslavement through acts of quiet resistance and open rebellion. The end of the Civil War brought emancipation. During the postwar period known as Reconstruction, the former slaves made tremendous progress in their journey from bondage to true freedom. They worked hard to restore their families and establish their economic independence. They built new schools, churches, and other institutions. They also struggled to secure their civil rights by forming political organizations, voting, and serving in government.

White southerners overwhelmingly opposed Reconstruction. Through fraud, intimidation, and violence, the former slave-holders strived to regain control of their state governments and

Opposite: A trainload of civil rights demonstrators arrive in the nation's capital for the 1963 March on Washington.

restore white supremacy. By the late 1800s, nearly all the gains that African Americans had made during Reconstruction had been erased. A new system known as Jim Crow had begun to take root across the United States, especially in the South. This complex set of laws and practices stripped blacks of their civil and political rights and provided for segregation in practically every area of public life.

Some African Americans responded to Jim Crow with a policy of compromise, or "accommodation." Instead of confronting the powerful forces of segregation, they worked to improve their lives within the boundaries of Jim Crow society. Other African Americans rejected accommodationism. They believed that the only way blacks would ever achieve their full rights as citizens was by fighting for them. W. E. B. DuBois, the leading opponent of accommodationism, declared that African Americans would demand "every single right that belongs to a freeborn American, political, civil, and social; and until we get these rights we will never cease to protest and assail the ears of America." In 1909 DuBois helped found the National Association for the Advancement of Colored People (NAACP). This organization would play a leading role in the struggle against the Jim Crow laws.

Linda Brown *(front)* was the subject of the landmark civil rights case *Brown* v. *Board of Education.*

Over time hundreds of other organizations joined the battle for civil rights, including the National Association of Colored Women, the National Urban League, and the Congress of Racial Equality. Black workers formed labor unions to fight for equal wages, working conditions, and job opportunities. Hundreds of thousands of African Americans who never joined a civil rights group or union supported the battle against Jim Crow by taking part in marches, boycotts, and other protests. By the early 1950s, all these efforts had begun to produce results. Boycotts had forced many white-owned businesses in northern cities to hire their first black employees. Baseball great Jackie Robinson had shattered the color barrier in professional sports. President Harry S. Truman had ordered the end of segregation in the armed forces. Most importantly, the 1954 Supreme Court ruling in the case of *Brown* v. *Board of Education* had declared that school segregation was unconstitutional.

Despite these victories, African Americans still faced a daily struggle against the Jim Crow system. They would have to work together like never before to overcome the forces arrayed against them. During the civil rights movement, their determination and courage would bring about a revolution that would shake the nation and transform American life forever.

A black-owned newspaper applauds the end of segregation in the armed forces in July 1948.

Rosa Parks is photographed in an Alabama jail, after her arrest for refusing to give up her bus seat for a white passenger.

Chapter 1

THE MONTGOMERY BUS BOYCOTT

ON DECEMBER 1, 1955, ROSA PARKS BOARDED A city bus in Montgomery, Alabama. The black seamstress was on her way home after a day's work at a downtown department store. She paid her fare. She got off the bus and walked to the "colored" door at the rear to get on again. Then she sat down in the middle of the bus, between the "whites-only" seats in the front and the "colored" seats in the back.

After a few stops, the white seats filled up. The driver told the four black passengers in the middle section of the bus to move. Three of them went to stand in the back of the bus. Rosa Parks kept her seat.

"Are you going to stand up?" the bus driver asked.

"No," Parks answered quietly.

At that, the angry driver left the bus. He returned with two police officers. They arrested the soft-spoken black woman for violating a city segregation law.

The modern civil rights movement had begun.

At the time of Rosa Parks's arrest, Jim Crow ruled in Montgomery, Alabama. In fact, racial segregation was a part of daily life all across the United States. Throughout the North, West, and Midwest, discriminatory practices restricted most African Americans to all-black city ghettos, black schools, and low-paying "colored" jobs. In the South, Jim Crow was the law of the land. Southern segregation laws required the separation of the races in practically every area of public life, from schools and restaurants to park benches and water fountains.

To the black citizens of Montgomery, one of the most infuriating areas of segregation was public transportation. Fewer blacks than whites owned cars. As a result, African Americans made up the majority of passengers on city buses. Nevertheless, black passengers had to sit at the back of the buses. When buses got crowded, they had to stand up to make room for the whites. "I work hard all day," complained one black working-woman in Montgomery, "and I had to stand up all the way home because I couldn't have a seat on the bus."

Blacks in Montgomery and elsewhere had made many attempts to oppose this discriminatory system. Hardly a week went by without the arrest of a black person somewhere in the South for refusing to give up his or her bus seat. None of these protests had made a difference, however. Leaders of the NAACP had concluded that the only way to end the segregation was to challenge it in court. They had been looking for a respectable community member who would make a good test case. Then they heard about Rosa Parks.

Many half-truths have crept into the story of the woman known as the Mother of the Civil Rights Movement. Some

Rosa Parks at work as a seamstress. The civil rights heroine would lose her job because of her stand against segregation.

accounts say that Parks refused to give up her seat simply because she was tired. In later years, she disputed that notion. "I was not tired physically," she said, "or no more tired than I usually was at the end of a working day. I was not old, although some people have an image of me as being old then." By the time she came to fame, the forty-two-year-old woman had already done a lot of thinking about discrimination. She had worked at the Montgomery branch of the NAACP, where she had witnessed many cases of racial injustice. Time after time she had seen those cases come to nothing because abused people were too intimidated to fight back. "No, the only tired I was," she explained, "was tired of giving in."

"THERE COMES A TIME"

As soon as Rosa Parks agreed to let the NAACP represent her in a test case against segregation, civil rights leaders went to work.

They distributed thousands of flyers announcing a boycott of city buses to protest Parks's arrest. The one-day boycott would take place on Monday, December 5, the day scheduled for her trial.

Monday morning the buses rolled through Montgomery nearly empty. Meanwhile, Rosa Parks went to trial. She was found guilty and ordered to pay fourteen dollars in fines and court costs. Her lawyers vowed to appeal the decision to a higher court.

That afternoon black leaders held a meeting. They formed a new organization, the Montgomery Improvement Association, to coordinate further protests. A twenty-six-year-old Baptist minister was appointed president of the MIA. The young pastor was chosen partly because he was new in town, so he had no enemies among the quarreling factions in Montgomery's black community. He was also an educated man, with a doctorate (an advanced degree) from Boston University. Furthermore, he was said to be an effective speaker. His name was Martin Luther King Jr.

Monday evening Dr. King addressed a mass rally at Montgomery's Holt Street Baptist Church. Thousands of people jammed the building. Thousands more stood outside, listening on loudspeakers. The crowd nodded and murmured approval as the young preacher delivered a hastily prepared speech that set the tone for the struggle that lay ahead.

> My friends, there comes a time when people get tired of being trampled over by the iron feet of oppression. . . . We are here this evening because we're tired now. And I want to say, that we are not here advocating violence. . . . The only weapon

that we have in our hands this evening is the weapon of protest. . . .

We are not wrong in what we are doing. If we are wrong, the Supreme Court of this nation is wrong. If we are wrong, the Constitution of the United States is wrong. If we are wrong, God Almighty is wrong. . . . If we are wrong, justice is a lie. . . . And we are determined here in Montgomery to work and fight until justice runs down like water.

WALKING FOR FREEDOM

The masses who had assembled at Holt Street Baptist Church voted to continue the boycott until the bus company met their demands. At first, those demands were modest. The Montgomery Improvement Association asked only that the company hire black bus drivers for routes in black neighborhoods, that all drivers treat black passengers courteously, and that passengers in

The black residents of Montgomery walk to work and school during the third month of their historic bus boycott.

THE POWER OF NONVIOLENCE

Martin Luther King Jr. believed that white Americans would never grant black Americans their rights without a fight. However, he was opposed to violence. A devout Christian, Dr. King believed in "turning the other cheek" and loving one's enemies. He had also been deeply impressed by the example of Indian leader Mohandas Gandhi, often known as Mahatma ("Great Soul") Gandhi. In the 1940s Mahatma Gandhi had used marches, sit-ins, boycotts, and other forms of "passive resistance" to win India's independence from Great Britain.

During the Montgomery bus boycott, King put his faith in nonviolent resistance to the test. He urged the black citizens of Montgomery to oppose the forces of segregation without hatred or bitterness. They must endure the violent attacks of segregationists without resorting to violence themselves. In this way, nonviolence would become a powerful weapon in the fight for civil rights, exposing the evils of racial oppression and stirring the con-

Martin Luther King stands before a portrait of Mahatma Gandhi, the Indian leader who helped inspire his commitment to nonviolence.

science of white America. "We shall match your capacity to inflict suffering by our capacity to endure suffering," King pledged to the enemies of black rights. "We'll wear you down . . . , and one day we will win our freedom. We will not only win freedom for ourselves, we will so appeal to your heart and conscience that we will win you in the process."

the rows between the white and black sections be seated on a first-come, first-served basis. All these requests were rejected.

In response, the black men, women, and children of Montgomery found other ways to get to school and work. They walked, sometimes for miles. They crowded into black-owned cars and taxis. Eventually the MIA organized an alternate transportation system. Black car owners donated their vehicles, and volunteer drivers picked up and dropped off passengers at sites throughout the city. The car-pool service carried about 30,000 people to and from work each day.

Montgomery's white citizens and city officials tried a variety of tactics to break up the boycott. Many employers threatened to fire their black employees. The police harassed volunteer drivers and car-pool riders. They arrested Martin Luther King and about one hundred other black leaders for violating an old state law restricting boycotts. Sometimes the white backlash turned violent. Dr. King's house and the homes of two other protest leaders were bombed, fortunately without injuries.

None of these tactics worked. Instead, persecution only increased the protesters' resolve. At one mass meeting in February 1956, a reporter watched as more than two thousand African Americans "chanted and sang, . . . shouted and prayed. . . . They pledged themselves again and again to 'passive resistance.'"

The harassment of protest leaders also helped attract widespread publicity for the boycott. Dozens of newspaper and television reporters went to Montgomery to cover the story. Donations and letters of support poured into the MIA office. Martin Luther King made the front page of the *New York Times* and the cover of *Time* magazine. The young minister was becoming an internationally known civil rights leader.

Coretta Scott King greets her husband on the steps of a Montgomery courthouse following his conviction on charges stemming from the bus boycott. Dr. King was released as his case went to appeal.

VICTORY!

By February 1956, the boycott had taken a toll on Montgomery's business community. The bus company had lost an estimated 65 percent of its income. Sales had dropped sharply at downtown stores as black customers did their shopping closer to home. White business owners were ready to grant the demands of the Montgomery Improvement Association. But city officials remained firm. The Jim Crow laws would remain in place.

The MIA's goals had grown along with the success of the boycott. Now the organization was demanding a complete end to bus segregation. In June a federal court ruled in favor of an MIA lawsuit against the bus company. The city of Montgomery appealed the decision, and the case went to the

THE CIVIL RIGHTS MOVEMENT

Supreme Court. In November the court issued its ruling. Segregation on buses operating within a state was unconstitutional.

The Montgomery bus boycott had lasted for more than a year. Tens of thousands of protesters welcomed the end of long walks, carpooling, and harassment. They were pleased that they could now sit wherever they wanted on city buses and expect to be treated with the same courtesy as white passengers. Most of all, they were thrilled by what they had achieved through strength and unity. "We had won self-respect," said civil rights leader Jo Ann Robinson.

> We felt that we were somebody, that somebody had to listen to us, that we had forced the white man to give what we knew was a part of our own citizenship. . . . If you have never had the feeling that this is not the other man's country . . . but that this is your country, too, then you don't know what I'm talking about. But it is a hilarious feeling that just goes all over you, that makes you feel that America is a great country and we're going to do more to make it greater.

African Americans in other southern cities followed the example of the Montgomery bus boycott, organizing their own nonviolent protests. In January 1957 black ministers from ten southern states met to form an organization to coordinate all the different demonstrations. Martin Luther King was elected president of the new Southern Christian Leadership Conference. Under his leadership, the SCLC would engage millions of ordinary people in a massive campaign for civil rights across the South.

Fourteen-year-old lynching victim Emmett Till

THE MURDER OF EMMETT TILL

The peaceful tactics of the Montgomery bus boycott were a sharp contrast to the violence used by white supremacists across the South to keep blacks "in their place." Four months before the boycott began, the nation had witnessed a particularly chilling demonstration of racial violence. Emmett Till, a fourteen-year-old boy from Chicago, had been visiting relatives in rural Money, Mississippi. One day Emmett hung out with a group of boys in front of a white-owned grocery store. Pulling a picture from his wallet, he bragged that he had a white girlfriend in Chicago. The local boys laughed in disbelief. They challenged Emmett to prove that he knew "how to handle white girls" by asking one for a date.

Unfamiliar with the Jim Crow world of the South, Emmett took the dare. Strutting into the grocery store, he bought some gum from the young white woman behind the counter. On his way out, he whistled at her and called, "Bye, baby." Three days later, the woman's husband and another man dragged Emmett from his bed. They beat him beyond recognition, shot him in the head, and threw his body into the Tallahatchie River.

The brutal murder of Emmett Till shocked the nation. Newspapers carried pictures of the boy's mutilated body. Hundreds of reporters covered the trial in which an all-white jury quickly cleared the two murderers of all charges. That verdict outraged civil rights supporters. It also

Emmett's grief-stricken mother, Mamie, vowed to turn her son's death into "a worldwide awakening that would change the course of history."

had a dramatic impact on an entire generation of young African Americans. John Lewis, who would become the leader of a student civil rights organization, recalled that Till's murder "galvanized [aroused] the country. A lot of us young black students in the South later on, we weren't sitting in for ourselves—we were sitting in for Emmett Till."

Chapter 2

The Little Rock Nine

AS AFRICAN AMERICANS MOURNED THE MURDER of Emmett Till and fought bus segregation in Montgomery, another civil rights battle was brewing. The 1954 Supreme Court decision in the case of *Brown* v. *Board of Education* had become a rallying point for segregationists. The court had ruled that school segregation was illegal. Opponents argued that the ruling violated the right of states to run their schools however they saw fit. Furthermore, many white southerners saw the *Brown* decision as an assault on the entire system of segregation. All across the South, segregationists vowed to resist this threat to the "southern way of life" by any means necessary.*

DELAYING TACTICS

Following the *Brown* decision, White Citizens' Councils sprang up throughout the South. The members of these white

*For more on *Brown* v. *Board of Education*, see volume 8 in this series, *Marching toward Freedom*.

Opposite: An angry mob jeers Elizabeth Eckford as she walks to her first day of classes at Central High School in Little Rock, Arkansas. Elizabeth was one of the nine courageous black students to take the first step toward school integration.

FAMOUS QUOTATIONS

JAMES F. BYRNES

"Frequently, the question is asked: 'Where do we go from here?' Solomon, with all his wisdom, could not give a positive answer. We do know that the approximately 40 million white Southerners will do everything that lawfully can be done to prevent the mixing of the races in the schools."

"Power intoxicates men. It is never voluntarily surrendered. It must be taken from them. The Supreme Court must be curbed."

SUPPORT THE
EDUCATIONAL FUND OF THE
CITIZENS' COUNCILS, Inc.
GREENWOOD, MISSISSIPPI

White Citizens' Councils sprang up across Mississippi after the 1954 Supreme Court decision outlawing school segregation.

supremacist groups included bankers, lawyers, school officials, ministers, and business owners. These "upstanding" citizens considered themselves more "respectable" than members of the Ku Klux Klan and other white terrorist organizations. Their aim was to fight desegregation not by violence but by "economic pressure." Any southerner, black or white, who supported integration risked losing his or her job or being denied credit at local banks and stores.

Although council members publicly renounced violence, their racist statements encouraged threats, intimidation, and sometimes attacks against blacks. Some council members secretly belonged to the Ku Klux Klan. To many critics, the White Citizens' Councils were nothing more than the Klan in suits instead of sheets.

Most southern politicians supported the White Citizens' Councils and the anti-integration campaign. In March 1956 one hundred southern congressmen issued a declaration denouncing the *Brown* decision. The "Southern Manifesto" warned that school desegregation would "destroy the system of public education." The declaration urged states to "resist forced integration by any lawful means."

The most common means used to resist integration was delay. The Supreme Court had ordered southern states to desegregate the public schools "with all deliberate speed." That vague timetable gave segregationists an excuse for dragging out the process. For years southern school districts continued to bar blacks from white schools, claiming that more speedy measures would lead to violence. Meanwhile, local officials redrew the maps of school districts and neighborhoods to ensure that black students remained in black schools. Many communities established all-white private schools, often funded with public money. In some cases school boards simply closed the schools rather than integrate them. Prince Edward County in Virginia, for example, closed down its entire public school system for five years, while state funds went to a series of white private academies.

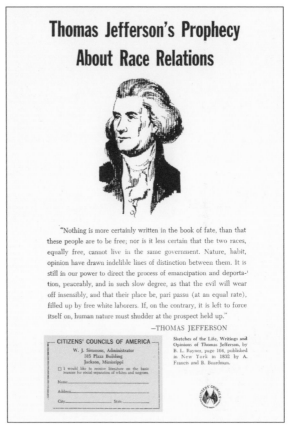

This White Citizens' Council newspaper ad quotes Thomas Jefferson in support of the segregation of the races.

It was only a matter of time before the conflict between the opponents and supporters of school desegregation came to a showdown. Both sides wondered how the federal government would respond when that happened. They got their answer in an unexpected place: the "moderate" southern city of Little Rock, Arkansas.

FIRST DAY OF SCHOOL

Compared with many other southern cities, Little Rock was racially progressive. The buses, parks, and police force in the Arkansas capital were integrated. The University of Arkansas Law School, located in Little Rock, had admitted its first black students without incident. After the *Brown* decision, the Little

A woman and child parade in front of the Arkansas Capitol to protest the planned integration of Little Rock's schools.

Rock school board had announced that it would comply with the ruling. By the time the board finished developing its desegregation plan, however, it was clear that Jim Crow had won the debate. Integration would be limited to a few "token" black students. The first small group would be admitted to all-white Central High School in 1957.

Racist whites opposed even this limited desegregation plan. Among the opponents was Arkansas governor Orval Faubus. The governor was up for reelection in 1958. He knew that he could win votes by appealing to segregationist views. When a group of white citizens went to court to try to block the integration of Central High, Faubus took their side. When a federal judge ordered the school to proceed with desegregation, the governor called out the Arkansas National Guard. He claimed that the guardsmen would be stationed at the school "to protect the lives and property of citizens." In reality, the troops were there to keep black students out.

On September 4, 1957, nine African-American teenagers prepared for their first day at Central High School. The "Little Rock Nine" knew that they would probably face some hostility in their new school. However, they all came from families that had always stressed the value of a good education, and Central High was one of the South's best high schools. "From the time I was two," recalled fifteen-year-old Melba Pattillo, "my mother said, 'You will go to college. Education is your key to survival,' and I understood that. It was a kind of curiosity, not an overwhelming desire to go to this school and integrate this school and change history."

Daisy Bates, president of the Arkansas NAACP, had arranged to drive the Little Rock Nine to school. Somehow that plan never reached fifteen-year-old Elizabeth Eckford. Elizabeth took a public bus to school. As she left the bus and headed toward Central High, a crowd of angry whites began to follow her, shouting threats and insults. The nervous girl reached the line of guardsmen standing outside the school. The soldiers blocked her way. When she tried to squeeze by, they raised their bayonets.

Frightened, Elizabeth turned and stumbled back toward the bus stop. The mob closed in, shouting, "Lynch her! Lynch her!" At last she reached the bus bench. "I don't think I could have gone another step," she said later. "I sat down

Racism showed its ugly face all across the South. These teenage girls are protesting the integration of schools in Montgomery, Alabama.

and the mob crowded up and began shouting all over again." Just then, two sympathetic white people forced their way through the surging mob. They sat with the terrified girl until the bus arrived and carried her to safety. Meanwhile, the other eight black students had arrived at Central High, only to be turned away by the armed guardsmen.

CRACKING THE WALL

Two weeks after the confrontation at Central High School, a federal judge ordered Governor Faubus to withdraw the National Guard. On September 23 the Little Rock Nine made their second attempt to enter the school. This time a crowd of about one thousand white men, women, and teenagers was waiting. The black students managed to slip through a side door. When word spread that they had made it inside the building, the mob erupted. Fearing a full-scale riot, the police decided to smuggle the students away to safety.

The next day President Dwight Eisenhower acted to enforce the Supreme Court's *Brown* decision. The president assumed command of the Arkansas National Guard. He also sent one thousand army paratroopers to Little Rock. A military convoy escorted the Little Rock Nine to Central High School. Armed soldiers marched them up the steps, then took up posts outside the building. This time the students were able to remain in school.

For the rest of the school year, National Guardsmen escorted the black students to and from school. During classes, armed soldiers patrolled the hallways. The soldiers could not be everywhere, however. While some of the white students at Central High were friendly, many others did their best to make

"WE WERE TRAPPED"

Melba Pattillo would never forget the day she and the other members of the Little Rock Nine first entered Little Rock's Central High School. After the black students slipped inside the building, the mob outside the building threatened to riot. Pattillo described the tense atmosphere as school officials and police devised a plan to rescue the trapped students.

I'd only been in the school a couple of hours and by that time it was apparent that the mob was just overrunning the school. Policemen were throwing down their badges and the mob was getting past the wooden sawhorses because the police would no longer fight their own in order to protect us. So we were all called into the principal's office, and there was great fear that we would not get out of this building. We were trapped. And I thought, Okay, so I'm going to die here, in school. . . .

A couple of kids, the black kids, that were with me were crying, and someone made a suggestion that if they allowed the mob to hang one kid, they could then get the rest out. And a gentleman, who I believed to be the police chief, said, "Unh-uh, how are you going to choose? You're going to let them draw straws?" He said, "I'll get them out." . . . We were put into two cars, grayish blue Fords. And the man instructed the drivers, he said, "Once you start driving, do not stop.". . . This guy revved up his engine and he came up out of the bowels of this building, and as he came up, I could just see hands reaching across this car, I could hear the yelling, I could see guns, and he was told not to stop. "If you hit somebody, you keep rolling, 'cause the kids are dead." And he did just that, and he didn't hit anybody. . . . He dropped me off at home. And I remember saying, "Thank you for the ride," and I should have said, "Thank you for my life."

Above: Melba Pattillo Beals at the 2005 unveiling of a monument at the Arkansas Capitol honoring the Little Rock Nine

National Guardsmen escort black students home after a day of classes at Central High School.

life miserable for their unwanted classmates. The black teenagers were spit on, called names, and tripped or kicked in the halls. Their books and lockers were vandalized. They were doused with ink in the classrooms, soup in the cafeteria, and scalding water in the gym shower rooms.

Mostly the teenagers tried to ignore their tormentors. On rare occasions they struck back. Sixteen-year-old Ernest Green, the only senior in the group, described the day Minniejean Brown took revenge on a white boy who had been following her around, calling, "Nigger, nigger, nigger." Ernest and Minnie were in the cafeteria. The girl "had just picked up her chili. . . . And before I could even say, 'Minnie, why don't you tell him to shut up,' Minnie had taken this chili, dumped it on this dude's head. There was just absolute silence in the place. And then the [cafeteria workers], all black, broke into applause."

That spring Ernest Green became Central High School's first black graduate. Martin Luther King attended the graduation ceremony, along with reporters from all over the country. Ernest was nervous as he crossed the auditorium stage, but he knew that "once I got as far as that principal and received that diploma, that I had cracked the wall. . . . When they called my name . . . there was this eerie silence. Nobody clapped. But I figured they didn't have to. Because after I got that diploma, that was it. I had accomplished what I had come there for."

Ernest Green prepares to make history by becoming the first black graduate of Central High School.

Ernest Green's graduation was just one small victory in the long war against Jim Crow. The following fall Governor Faubus closed all of Little Rock's high schools for a year rather than proceed with desegregation. When the Supreme Court forced the doors to reopen, the Little Rock school board used a variety of means, legal and illegal, to delay integration. It would be more than ten years before all of Little Rock's public schools were integrated. Desegregation also proceeded at a snail's pace at other schools throughout the South. Meanwhile, an entire generation of young African Americans was taking the battle for civil rights to a new front: the South's segregated lunch counters.

Four black college students sit at a whites-only lunch counter in Greensboro, North Carolina. Franklin McCain is seated second from left.

Chapter 3

SIT-INS AND FREEDOM RIDES

ON FEBRUARY 1, 1960, FOUR COLLEGE FRESHMEN sat down at the lunch counter in a Woolworth's variety store in Greensboro, North Carolina. They asked for coffee. The waitress replied, "We don't serve coloreds here." The young men showed the woman the school supplies they had just bought. Why would Woolworth's serve blacks at one counter, they asked, and deny them service at another?

The waitress called for the store manager. He asked the four students to leave. They politely refused. Then a police officer entered the store. The man paced up and down, knocking his nightstick against his hand. He looked "mean and red and a little bit upset and a little bit disgusted," recalled one of the students, Franklin McCain. "You had the feeling that he didn't know what the hell to do." The officer was angered by the students' actions, "but we [hadn't] provoked him outwardly enough for him to resort to violence."

The four students stayed until the store closed. Then they filed out, promising to return the next day. "If it's possible to know what it means to have your soul cleansed—I felt pretty clean at that time," said McCain. "I felt as though I had gained my manhood. . . . I felt as though the manhood of a number of other black persons had been restored and had gotten some respect from just that one day."

STUDENTS TAKE THE LEAD

The Greensboro sit-in marked the beginning of a new stage in the civil rights movement. A new generation of African Americans was coming of age. These young men and women were tired of the slow pace of progress in school desegregation and other civil rights reforms. They wanted change. They wanted it *now*. And they were willing to put their own lives on the line to challenge the Jim Crow system.

Franklin McCain, Joseph McNeil, David Richmond, and Ezell Blair Jr.—the four young men known as the Greensboro Four—had spent many hours discussing segregation. At last, they had decided that it was time for action. In planning their protest, they had looked to the examples set by Mahatma Gandhi, Martin Luther King, Rosa Parks, and the young black students in Little Rock. The four freshmen had decided that they, too, would use nonviolent action as a weapon against injustice.

On February 2 the Greensboro Four returned to Woolworth's as promised. With them were more than twenty classmates. The next day the group had swelled to more than sixty. By the fifth day, more than three hundred students were taking turns sitting at the lunch counter, while waitresses ignored them and reporters watched them. Among the black demonstrators were a few white students from a nearby women's college. One young white woman told reporters that she felt a "moral obligation" to support the black freedom fighters.

As the sit-in movement grew, it was also spreading. Within a week of the first Greensboro protests, students were staging sit-ins at segregated lunch counters in neighboring Durham and Winston-Salem, North Carolina. Within a month, the protests would expand to college towns in South Carolina, Virginia, Tennessee, and Florida. By the end of 1960, an estimated 70,000 students, both black and white, would take part in sit-ins in dozens of cities in every southern state. The Greensboro Four's simple act of resistance had sparked a challenge to Jim Crow throughout the South.

A young activist trains for a nonviolent demonstration by learning to endure harassment without fighting back.

LESSONS IN NONVIOLENCE

Students in Nashville, Tennessee, had begun planning their own sit-ins months before the Greensboro protests. Hundreds of young men and women had attended nonviolence workshops led by James Lawson, a divinity student and civil rights activist. "We would do things like pretend we were sitting in at lunch counters," recalled Diane Nash, who was a sophomore at Nashville's Fisk University. "We would practice things such as how to protect your head from a beating. . . . We would practice not striking back if someone struck us."

When word of the Greensboro Four reached Nashville, the students decided that it was time to put their training into action. On February 13, 1960, more than one hundred young men and women began sit-ins at segregated lunch counters in downtown Nashville. For the first two weeks, the protests proceeded peacefully. Then the white backlash began.

John Lewis was part of the group assigned to Nashville's Woolworth's on February 27. As the students entered the store, a crowd of young white men began to shout, "Go home, nigger!" Lewis sat down at the counter. He was "hit in the ribs, not too hard, but enough to knock me over. Down the way I could see one of the white men stubbing a lit cigarette against the back of a guy in our group. . . . I got back on my stool and sat there, not saying a word. The others did the same." Meanwhile, at another Nashville store, "mustard was squeezed onto the head of one black male student. . . . Ketchup was poured down the shirt of another." A white student who had joined the pro-

A protester who has been sprayed with ketchup continues his sit-in at a lunch counter in Jackson, Mississippi.

testers "was pulled off his stool, beaten and kicked." Finally, the police arrived. Ignoring the white attackers, the officers arrested the peaceful protesters for "disorderly conduct."

Television cameras had captured the events in Nashville. Over the following days and weeks, TV and newspapers would spread the news of attacks on student protesters in other southern cities. Many Americans across the nation were sickened by the violence. Even white southerners could not help noticing the contrast between the polite, neatly dressed demonstrators and the thugs who taunted and harassed them.

Southern whites were also feeling the economic effects of the student protests. The sit-ins disrupted business. In many areas black customers had begun to boycott stores in support of the young demonstrators. White businessmen and women facing thousands of dollars in lost sales were becoming desperate. In March 1960, San Antonio, Texas, became the first southern city to desegregate its lunch counters. Two months later, Nashville followed. By the end of the year, at least eighty other southern towns and cities would open their lunch counters to black customers.

THE FREEDOM RIDERS

In 1961 young black activists turned their energies to another area in the civil rights struggle: interstate transportation. African Americans who traveled from state to state in the South were forced to ride in the back of buses. They were barred from whites-only waiting rooms, restrooms, and restaurants in southern bus terminals. Those practices were against the law. Fifteen years earlier, the Supreme Court had banned segregation on interstate buses. In 1960 it had extended the ban to bus terminals. James Farmer, director of the Congress of Racial Equality (CORE), decided that it was time to put the court's rulings to the test.

The first Freedom Riders left Washington, D.C., on May 4, 1961. The interracial group included thirteen volunteers from CORE and another civil rights group, the Student Nonviolent Coordinating Committee. Their plan was simple. Dividing into two groups, they would board two regularly scheduled segregated buses leaving Washington for New Orleans, Louisiana. The

"BIGGER THAN A HAMBURGER"

The civil rights movement could not have succeeded with-out the work of strong, dedicated black women. One of these unsung heroines was Ella Baker. Born and raised in the Jim Crow South, Baker was passionately committed to the cause of equal rights for all people: black and white, rich and poor, male and female. In 1938 she went to work for the NAACP. She spent several years helping southern black communities organize and fight for civil rights. Later she became one of the founders and direc-tors of the Southern Christian Leadership Conference.

Baker was impressed by the student sit-ins in Nashville and other southern cities. In April 1960 she organized a conference where the leaders of all the different protests could get together and coordinate future actions. Older civil rights leaders attend-ing the conference wanted to take charge of the student movement. The young activists wanted to remain independent. Baker sided with the students. She encour-aged them to hold on to their vision and never let anyone, especially the "older folks," tell them what to do. She also warned the young activists that a long road lay before them. The fight for civil rights meant "something much bigger than a hamburger or even a giant-sized Coke." Breaking down the barriers to black rights in areas such as voting, education, and the workplace would be much tougher than integrating lunch counters.

With Baker's encouragement, the student leaders formed the Student Nonvio-lent Coordinating Committee, or SNCC (pronounced "snick"). Dedicated to fighting racial discrimination through nonviolent action, SNCC would become a major force in the civil rights movement. While the group remained independent of older civil rights organizations, it did have one "adult adviser": Ella Baker.

Ella Baker was an important behind-the-scenes civil rights organizer.

Freedom Riders would take their seats just like the other passengers, except for one notable difference: blacks and whites would sit together. When the buses stopped, they would use the bus terminal facilities, ignoring any WHITE and COLORED signs. The riders knew that crossing the color line would probably provoke violence, especially as they went deeper into the South. By putting their safety at risk, they hoped to shine a spotlight on Jim Crow and pressure the federal government to enforce the antisegregation laws.

The first trouble came in South Carolina. When a black Freedom Rider tried to enter the whites-only waiting room at the Rock Hill bus terminal, a gang of white youths punched and kicked him and his white companion. A few days later, the lead bus reached Anniston, Alabama. Two hundred angry whites armed with knives, clubs, and iron pipes were

Freedom Riders gather outside their burning bus near Anniston, Alabama, on May 14, 1961.

waiting in the terminal. The mob surrounded the bus, banging on the windows and slashing the tires. As the bus escaped from the town, the mob gave chase. Six miles outside Anniston, someone hurled a firebomb through the rear window. The passengers managed to exit the bus just before the fuel tank exploded.

Meanwhile, the riders in the second bus were also in grave danger. When they reached Anniston, a group of white men took over the bus. They drove on to Birmingham, Alabama. There a reporter traveling with the Freedom Riders watched in horror as "toughs grabbed the passengers into alleys and corridors, pounding them with pipes, with key rings, and with fists. One passenger was knocked down at my feet by twelve of the hood-lums, and his face was beaten and kicked until it was a bloody pulp." It would take fifty-three stitches to close the gashes in the man's head. Another rider was beaten so badly that he would remain paralyzed for the rest of his life.

The bus drivers refused to take the passengers any farther. The remaining Freedom Riders flew on to New Orleans. They were bruised and battered but not defeated.

A BLOODY FIGHT

James Farmer wanted to call off the Freedom Rides. SNCC leaders in Nashville said no. The students believed that backing down "would effectively end the entire civil rights movement," recalled John Lewis. "It would tell those in the South . . . that violence *can* put an end to peaceful protest."

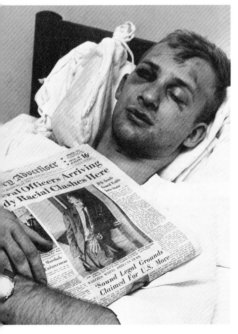

Freedom Rider Jim Zwerg lies in a hospital bed after being beaten by a white mob in Montgomery, Alabama.

In May student activists headed from Nashville to Birmingham to resume the Freedom Rides where they had ended. The riders took a bus to Montgomery, Alabama. There they were met by hundreds of angry white men and women. The mob assaulted the students. They also attacked reporters covering the story and a federal official who had been sent as an observer by President John F. Kennedy.

Throughout the Freedom Rides, Kennedy had been reluctant to intervene on the side of the protesters. The president needed the support of southern voters and legislators, and the quickest way to lose that support was to take a stand against segregation. But the racial turmoil in the South was becoming increasingly embarrassing. After the assault in Montgomery, Kennedy finally moved to prevent further violence. He sent six hundred federal

National Guardsmen escort Freedom Riders on the last leg of their journey to Mississippi in May 1961.

marshals to Alabama and pressured the governor to call out the National Guard. Four days later, twenty-seven Freedom Riders boarded buses in Montgomery, along with a host of reporters and guardsmen. This time they made it to Mississippi. When they arrived in Jackson, they were arrested and sentenced to sixty days' hard labor in a Mississippi prison camp.

The imprisonment of the Freedom Riders did not stop the protests. Volunteers continued to pour into Montgomery from college campuses all across the country. By the end of the summer, more than three hundred riders had been jailed. Still they kept coming. The students rode buses through nearly every state in the South. Their courage and suffering captured the nation's attention. Millions of white Americans who had followed the story through newspapers, radio, and television witnessed the brutality of racism for the first time in their lives.

In November 1961 the Kennedy administration bowed to public pressure and issued regulations enforcing integration in interstate travel. The Freedom Riders had triumphed. But for activists such as John Lewis, the "work was just beginning. . . . If there was anything I learned on that long, bloody bus trip of 1961, it was this—that we were in for a long, bloody fight here in the American South."

Chapter 4

The Battle in Birmingham

IN DECEMBER 1961 A COALITION OF CIVIL RIGHTS groups launched an ambitious campaign in Albany, Georgia. Under the leadership of the Southern Christian Leadership Conference (SCLC) and the Student Nonviolent Coordinating Committee (SNCC), Albany's black citizens staged sit-ins, boycotts, marches, and other protests against the segregation of public facilities. Hundreds of people were arrested. Among them was Martin Luther King, who went to jail three times in support of the Albany Movement.

After months of protest, very little had changed in Albany. City officials had refused to negotiate with movement leaders. They had shut down the buses, parks, and libraries rather than integrate them. In August 1962 Dr. King and other discouraged SCLC leaders left Albany, and the mass demonstrations ended. Some people called the Albany Movement the worst failure of King's civil rights career.

Opposite: Martin Luther King Jr. sits in a jail cell in Birmingham, Alabama.

To the black citizens of Albany, however, the movement was not a failure. Over the following months, they would face a violent backlash from local whites. In response, they would regroup and fight even harder against segregation. William Anderson, the local doctor who directed the Albany Movement, observed "a change in the attitude of the people. . . . They had made a determination within their own minds that they would never accept that segregated society as it was, anymore."

Just as importantly, the Albany Movement had served as a training ground for civil rights activists. Black leaders realized that they had not planned the campaign carefully enough. They had failed to set clear goals and work together effectively to achieve them. They would put those lessons to good use as they prepared for the next major battleground in the civil rights struggle: Birmingham, Alabama.

Birmingham Police Chief "Bull" Connor became a symbol of racism for his violent suppression of civil rights.

"BOMBINGHAM"

In 1963 civil rights leaders considered Birmingham the "worst big city in America." Every area of public life in Birmingham was strictly segregated. Every attempt to stand up for African-American rights was quickly and brutally repressed. Ku Klux Klan members and sympathizers were part of the city's government, courts, and police department. Eugene "Bull" Connor, the head of the police and fire departments, was a vicious racist who would stop at nothing to enforce segregation. Since the end of World War II, there had been so many bombings of black homes and churches in Birmingham that

FREEDOM SONGS

In Albany, Georgia, freedom songs became a vital part of the civil rights movement. Protestors sang these inspirational songs as they picketed outside Albany's stores and marched in the city streets. They sang to keep their spirits up as they shivered in prison cells. For student activist Bernice Johnson, singing released "a force and power within myself I had never heard before. . . . After the song, the differences among us would not be as great."

Many freedom songs were old hymns or spirituals with new words added to fit the time and place. Others were composed especially for the movement. "We Shall Overcome" was adapted from a union song of the 1940s, which itself was derived from a hymn. Simple, hopeful lyrics and a majestic melody made this song the unofficial anthem of the civil rights movement.

Folk singer Bob Dylan on the back porch of the SNCC office in Greenwood, Mississippi

*We shall overcome
We shall overcome
We shall overcome someday.
Oh, deep in my heart
I do believe
We shall overcome someday.* *

*You can listen to performances of "We Shall Overcome" by folksinger Pete Seeger and rock singer Bruce Springsteen at http://www.npr.org/templates/story/story.php?storyId=5362968

many people called the city "Bombingham." Not surprisingly, none of these crimes had ever been punished.

Early in 1963 Martin Luther King and other SCLC officials met with Birmingham minister and activist Fred Shuttlesworth. Together the leaders mapped out a civil rights campaign that would involve the city's entire black community. Their goal was the desegregation of public facilities. Their target was the white business community. Through protests that deprived downtown store owners of their black customers and scared away white customers, the activists would force the merchants to grant their demands.

The campaign was launched during the busy Easter shopping season. On April 3 protesters staged sit-ins at segregated lunch counters in downtown Birmingham. Store owners responded by closing their lunch counters to all customers.

A police dog attacks a teenage demonstrator during a peaceful march in Birmingham.

The organizers moved on to mass marches. On April 6 about forty protesters marched on Birmingham's City Hall and were arrested. The next day police used nightsticks and attack dogs to scatter the marchers. After that, an Alabama judge issued a restraining order forbidding Martin Luther King and other black leaders from taking part in the demonstrations.

Protest leaders were getting discouraged. The Birmingham campaign was not drawing as much support as they had hoped from the black community. Most of the volunteers were in jail, and few people were left to take their place on the streets. Meanwhile, newspaper and television reporters were ignoring the protests. Martin Luther King decided that it was time for a personal act of defiance. Two days before Easter, he led another march on City Hall and was thrown in jail.

Dr. King's arrest attracted national attention. It also inspired a group of Alabama clergymen to publish an open letter in a local newspaper. The white ministers called on African Americans to show more patience and "common sense" in pressing their demands. King read the statement in his jail cell. He began to scribble a reply in the margins of the newspaper. His famous "Letter from a Birmingham Jail" explained his people's "legitimate and unavoidable impatience" for justice. "I guess it is easy," he wrote,

> for those who have never felt the stinging darts of segregation to say, "Wait." But when you have seen the vicious mobs lynch your mothers and fathers at will and drown your sisters and brothers at whim; when you have seen hate-filled policemen curse, kick, brutalize and even kill your black brothers and sisters . . . ; when you see the vast majority of your twenty million Negro brothers smothering in an airtight cage of poverty . . . ; when you are humiliated day in and day out by nagging signs reading "white" and "colored"; . . . then you will understand why we find it difficult to wait.

Birmingham school-children are led to jail after taking part in a civil rights demonstration.

THE CHILDREN'S CRUSADE

After Dr. King was released from jail, the Birmingham campaign entered its last and most dramatic stage. Thousands of young African Americans had been watching their elders' non-violent protests. They knew that they had a personal stake in the fight against segregation, and they wanted to do their share. On May 2 nearly a thousand black boys and girls marched toward the downtown business district, singing freedom songs. More than six hundred children, ranging in age from six to eighteen, were arrested.

The following day Bull Connor called out the fire department. As another one thousand young people began to march, the firemen turned on their high-pressure hoses. The force of the water blasted the children off their feet. Many were flushed down the street, slamming into walls and parked cars. Then the police attacked the children and bystanders who tried to defend them. The officers swung their nightsticks, while police dogs

THE CIVIL RIGHTS MOVEMENT

tore into the protesters' flesh and clothes.

That night millions of Americans, black and white, gasped in horror as they watched the violence on TV. Stories of the mistreatment of the children jailed in Birmingham added to the outrage. President Kennedy denounced the "shameful scenes" and sent federal officials to help negotiate an end to the conflict.

On May 10 Birmingham's black leaders and white business-people reached an agreement. The store owners would desegregate all lunch counters, restrooms, fitting rooms, and water fountains. They would also begin to hire African Americans as clerks and salespeople.

The Birmingham campaign marked a turning point for the black freedom struggle. The nation had seen young Americans brutalized for peacefully demanding their rights as citizens. For the first time, a large segment of the public favored new civil rights legislation. The Kennedy administration also seemed ready to back up the civil rights movement. A day after the Birmingham agreement, two bombs meant for black leaders exploded in the city. No one was injured, but the attacks prompted an angry demonstration and further police brutality. President Kennedy quickly sent in federal troops to restore order. "The Birmingham agreement was and is a fair and just accord," the president said. "The federal government will not permit it to be sabotaged."

A Dream and a Tragedy

The spring and summer of 1963 saw what *Time* magazine described as a "feverish, fragmented, almost uncontrollable revolution." In nearly every large town and city in the South, African Americans engaged in nonviolent demonstrations

Ten-year-old Darrell Evers sits with his mother, Myrlie, at the funeral of his father, civil rights leader Medgar Evers.

against segregation. They staged sit-ins and boycotts. They marched through the streets and rallied outside courthouses and city halls. In one city after another, white officials negotiated with the demonstrators. By the end of the year, more than three hundred southern cities would agree to some form of integration.

At the same time, racist whites in many southern cities did their best to suppress the black uprising. On June 11 NAACP leader Medgar Evers was gunned down outside his home in Jackson, Mississippi. That same day Alabama governor George Wallace stood in a doorway at the University of Alabama, barring the school's first black students from entering. Wallace was finally forced to step aside by Alabama National Guardsmen acting under orders from President Kennedy. One week later, police used nightsticks, fire hoses, and tear gas to break up civil rights demonstrations in Danville, Virginia, and Savannah, Georgia. Other bloody clashes would take place between black protesters and law enforcement officers in Cambridge, Maryland; Gadsden, Alabama; Americus, Georgia; and the Harlem section of New York City. To many Americans, it seemed as though the country was on the brink of a racial civil war.

Amid all this turmoil, civil rights leaders were planning a massive March on Washington. The march would include black and white members of nearly every civil rights organization. It would demonstrate the rising tide of public support for the black freedom struggle. Organizers hoped that this powerful public display would help ensure passage of a new Civil Rights Act that President Kennedy had sent to Congress.

Nearly a quarter of a million people took part in the March on Washington. On August 28, 1963, they gathered before the Lincoln Memorial as Martin Luther King delivered what would become his most famous speech.

A black-owned newspaper covers the 1963 March on Washington. The smaller headline reflects Myrlie Evers's commitment to continue her late husband's fight for racial equality.

I say to you, my friends, that even though we must face the difficulties of today and tomorrow, I still have a dream. It is a dream deeply rooted in the American dream that one day this nation will rise up and live out the true meaning of its creed: "We hold these truths to be self-evident, that all men are created equal."

I have a dream that one day on the red hills of Georgia, sons of former slaves and sons of former slave owners will be able to sit down together at the table of brotherhood. . . .

I have a dream that my four little children will one day live in a nation where they will not be judged by the color of their skin but by the content of their character. I have a dream today!

Dr. King's audience shared his dream that the long dark days of Jim Crow were nearly behind them. A few weeks later, those hopes were shattered. On September 15, 1963, white segregationists bombed the Sixteenth Street Baptist Church in Birmingham. Sunday school had just let out. Four young black girls were killed. The tragedy was graphic proof that African Americans still had a long way to go to overcome the terrible forces of white supremacy.

Chapter 5

MISSISSIPPI FREEDOM SUMMER

ON NOVEMBER 22, 1963, PRESIDENT JOHN F. Kennedy was assassinated in Dallas, Texas. African Americans mourned the death of the young president. They also worried that the tragedy might mean the end of the Civil Rights Act. But Kennedy's successor, Lyndon B. Johnson, quickly made it clear that he supported civil rights legislation. President Johnson proposed an even stronger bill and worked hard to push it through Congress.

On July 2, 1964, Johnson signed the Civil Rights Act of 1964. The new law banned discrimination in employment and federally assisted programs. It also outlawed segregation in public facilities such as hotels, restaurants, and movie theaters.

One area where the Civil Rights Act fell short was voting rights. For nearly a century, white southerners had used a variety of tactics to maintain their hold on political power. Black voter applicants were required to fill out long, complicated forms. They had to pass ridiculously hard "literacy tests." In

Opposite: A CORE volunteer encourages a resident of a poor neighborhood in Mississippi to register to vote.

addition to these hurdles, southern blacks who tried to register to vote faced harassment, threats, and sometimes violence.

No state had a worse record on voting rights than Mississippi. Only about 5 percent of the state's eligible African Americans were registered to vote. Dedicated civil rights volunteers had been working against incredible odds to correct that injustice. In the summer of 1964, their efforts would focus the nation's attention on Mississippi.

THE VOTING RIGHTS CAMPAIGN

Robert Moses was an unlikely hero. The young high school math teacher was once described as "frail, bespectacled, and soft-spoken to the point of whispering." Beneath that quiet exterior, however, were a courage and a determination that would make Moses one of the most important voices in the civil rights movement.

Moses had joined the Student Nonviolent Coordinating Committee in 1960. The following year, he gave up his teaching career in New York and went to Mississippi to organize a voter registration drive. White Mississippians were maintaining their supremacy over blacks through a brutal system of intimidation and violence. Moses knew that the key to overcoming that oppression was the vote. Only by gaining political power would black Mississippians ever force whites to grant them equality and justice.

Robert Moses was a key leader of the campaign to register black voters in Mississippi.

During the summer and fall of 1961, Robert Moses and a small group of SNCC volunteers went door-to-door in McComb, Mississippi, getting acquainted with black residents. The young civil rights workers forged strong ties with local black leaders who had been trying to fight Jim Crow on their own. Together, the "outside agitators" and local activists encouraged McComb's black citizens to fill out the complicated voter registration forms. Then the volunteers escorted a few brave men and women to the county courthouse, where the applicants tried to register to vote.

White segregationists—including local government leaders, the police, and members of the White Citizens' Council and Ku Klux Klan—responded to the voter registration drive with violence. Robert Moses was beaten nearly unconscious with the butt of a knife. Other SNCC volunteers and black Mississippians were threatened, jailed, whipped, and beaten. Herbert Lee, a local farmer involved in voter registration, was shot and killed.

The harsh attacks only strengthened the volunteers' commitment. In 1962 SNCC and other civil rights groups operating in Mississippi joined forces to form the Council of Federated Organizations (COFO). Under the leadership of Robert Moses, COFO workers expanded the voter registration drive to ten Mississippi counties.

The increased activity led to a new wave of terror. COFO workers and local black leaders were harassed, beaten, and killed. The homes and churches of black activists were burned. In the face of this reign of terror, the Mississippi voter registration campaign nearly ground to a halt. After two years of hard work, the number of registered black voters in the state had barely budged. It was time for a bold new plan.

MISSISSIPPI BURNING

In November 1963 COFO workers staged a Freedom Vote in Mississippi. More than 83,000 African Americans across the state cast their ballots for pro-civil rights candidates in the mock election. White segregationists in Mississippi had been arguing that blacks were simply too lazy and unintelligent to vote. The large turnout proved that their claim was a lie.

About eighty white students from northern colleges had helped organize the Freedom Vote. Thanks to their presence, newspapers across the country had covered the election. That gave Robert Moses an idea. He proposed a massive new campaign involving up to one thousand northern students. The volunteers would take part in Mississippi Freedom Summer, a statewide program of political education, organization, and voter registration. Their participation "would make it abundantly clear that this is not a situation which can be ignored any longer."

The first group of volunteers arrived in June 1964. Nearly all the recruits were white college students from well-to-do families. They had gone through a weeklong training program. Experienced COFO workers had taught them the skills they would need to protect themselves against racist attacks. Still, the young students were unprepared for the hostility they would face in Mississippi.

On June 21 three volunteers went missing. Andrew Goodman and Michael Schwerner, white students from New York, and James Chaney, a native black Mississippian, had been investigating a church burning near the small town of Philadelphia, Mississippi. The local sheriff had arrested them. After a few hours, they were released. The three young men drove away from the jail. After that, they vanished.

The disappearances made headlines across the nation. The widespread media attention forced the FBI to launch a serious investigation, code-named Mississippi Burning. In August a paid informer led agents to the bodies of the slain men. Ku Klux Klansmen working in league with the police had shot the three civil

THE RACIAL DIVIDE

Some COFO workers opposed the recruit-
ment of large numbers of white volunteers
for Mississippi Freedom Summer. They
were afraid that local blacks who had begun
to think and act for themselves might fall
into the habit of letting the well-educated,
well-to-do whites make decisions for them.
When the northerners went back home, the
people in Mississippi would have to start all
over again.

COFO leaders Ed King *(left)* and Aaron Henry over-
came racial barriers to work together in the struggle
for civil rights.

These concerns led to conflicts between
the white volunteers and the black activists
assigned to train them. During one training
session, the organizers showed the new
recruits a television documentary about
racism. A fat, red-necked voting official was
explaining in a southern drawl why "nigras"
didn't want to vote.

"It seemed to us, the young white college students," recalled nineteen-year-old
Robbie Osman of New York City, "that
this guy was as ridiculous, as pathetic . . .
a racist as we ever expected to see. And
we laughed."

The students' laughter infuriated the civil
rights veterans, who knew that the racist
official was anything but a joke. "How can
we put our lives on the line with you guys?"
one black trainer asked the recruits. "Maybe
you won't laugh when you meet these guys
and hear them talk and know that they are
doing it every day."

"I think it was a moment," said Osman,
"in which we all had to stop and realize the
gap between us. If we were to reach across
it, it was gonna take a lot of reaching."

Exchanges such as these led to greater
understanding and cooperation between
the northern volunteers and Mississippi
activists. The two groups would work
together closely under stressful and
dangerous conditions during Freedom
Summer. The underlying tensions between
them, however, would never completely
disappear.

From left to right: Michael Schwerner, James Chaney, and Andrew Goodman. The three civil rights volunteers were murdered by Mississippi Ku Klux Klansmen in 1964.

rights workers and buried their bodies at a construction site.*

The murders were just the beginning of a campaign of terror that would rock Mississippi all through Freedom Summer. Over the course of two months, white segregationists would counter the "northern invasion" with at least six killings, thirty-five shootings, and sixty-five burnings and bombings.

THE MISSISSIPPI FREEDOM DEMOCRATIC PARTY

Intimidation and violence could not stop Freedom Summer. Altogether about one thousand northern volunteers went south to help build a better life for Mississippi blacks. These dedicated young men and women set up community centers where local blacks could obtain basic legal and medical services. They established Freedom Schools, where thousands of poor black children got their first chance for a decent education. These innovative schools taught not only reading, writing, and math but also African-American history, race relations, and political leadership. The young teachers emphasized student participation instead of traditional methods such as memorization. The goal of the Freedom Schools, explained Robert Moses, was to give "the young people in Mississippi . . . a forum in which they could really think through and discuss problems which were really important for them."

*In 1967 seven white Mississippians were found guilty of violating the civil rights of the slain men and sentenced to short prison terms. Years later, the case was reopened. In 2005 former Ku Klux Klan leader Edgar Ray Killen was convicted of organizing the murders and sentenced to sixty years in prison.

The most dramatic achievement of Mississippi Freedom Summer was the creation of the Mississippi Freedom Democratic Party (MFDP). African Americans were excluded from the state's "regular," all-white Democratic Party. MFDP was established to give them a voice in their government. All through the summer of 1964, volunteers across Mississippi worked to register black voters. At the same time, they signed up thousands of members for the new party.

Two boys help out in a Mississippi civil rights office during the 1964 voter registration drive.

In August 1964 the Mississippi Freedom Democratic Party sent its own elected delegates to the Democratic National Convention in Atlantic City. The MFDP delegates challenged the right of the "regular" Democrats to represent Mississippi. Fannie Lou Hamer (see page 61) argued their case before a Democratic committee. Her plainspoken, moving account of the ordeals she had suffered working for voting rights was televised to a nationwide audience. For many Americans, it was a first inside look at the brutality of racial oppression in Mississippi.

In the end Democratic leaders offered the MFDP two honorary seats, without voting rights, at the convention. The delegates rejected the "back of the bus" compromise and were barred from the convention. The Democrats went on to nominate Lyndon Johnson, who would win election to his first full term as president.

A New Era

As Freedom Summer came to an end, weary civil rights workers looked back on their failures and successes. Many young black activists remained bitter about the treatment of MFDP delegates at the Democratic National Convention. Their resentment would lead these activists to a new militarism. According to SNCC worker Cleveland Sellers, young activists stopped believing "that our task was exposing injustices so that the 'good' people of America could eliminate them. . . . The movement had turned into something else. After Atlantic City, our struggle was not for civil rights, but for liberation."

Other civil rights workers viewed Mississippi Freedom Summer as an important step forward in the march toward true freedom. The poor and oppressed blacks of Mississippi had told their story before a national audience at the Democratic convention. Four years later, the MFDP would again challenge the all-white Mississippi delegation. This time, they would win. Mississippi would send its first integrated delegation to the 1968 Democratic convention. When Fannie Lou Hamer took her seat as an official delegate, she received a standing ovation.

Meanwhile, the lives of thousands of black Mississippians had been changed forever. "Freedom Summer was the beginning of a whole new era," said Unita Blackwell of Mayersville, Mississippi.

> People began to feel that they wasn't just helpless anymore, that they had come together. Black and white had come from the North and the West and even from some cities in the South. . . . They came to talk about that we had a right to register to vote, we had a right to stand up for our rights. That's a whole new era for us.

FANNIE LOU HAMER

Fannie Lou Hamer's life changed forever on August 26, 1962. That was the day the Mississippi sharecropper's wife attended a mass meeting at her church. Organizers for the SCLC and SNCC asked for volunteers to go down to the county courthouse and register to vote. Hamer raised her hand. "I guess if I'd had any sense I'd a been a little scared," she later said. "The only thing they could do to me was kill me and it seemed like they'd been trying to do that a little bit at a time ever since I could remember."

When Hamer returned from the courthouse, she met her employer, who was also the owner of the plantation where she and her family lived. "We're not going to have this in Mississippi," the white man said. "If you don't withdraw you will have to leave." Hamer left the plantation that night. She joined SNCC and went to work registering other black Mississippians.

Fannie Lou Hamer's courageous stand brought harassment from local white businesspeople and the police. No one would hire anyone in her family. Her husband was arrested for failing to pay a $9,000 water bill—despite the fact that their house had no running water.

The worst ordeal came in June 1963, when Hamer and several other SNCC workers were returning from a voter registration workshop. The highway patrol stopped their bus in Winona, Mississippi. Hamer was taken to the county jail, where she was brutally beaten. She suffered permanent injuries as a result of the abuse.

In 1964 Fannie Lou Hamer helped found the Mississippi Freedom Democratic Party. She went on to serve as a delegate from Mississippi at the 1968 Democratic National Convention. Throughout her life she would spread the message that African Americans had to depend on themselves, not anyone else, to ensure their rights.

Above: Fannie Lou Hamer at the Democratic National Convention in August 1964.

Chapter 6

To the Mountaintop

IN LATE 1964 MARTIN LUTHER KING AND OTHER SCLC leaders met to plan their next move in the civil rights campaign. They decided to keep the focus on voting rights. The events of Mississippi Freedom Summer had made it clear that new legislation was needed to guarantee southern blacks the right to register and vote.

They would make their case in Selma, Alabama. African Americans made up about half of the small city's population, but only about 1 percent were registered to vote. Amelia Boynton, head of a local civil rights group, had been trying to register black voters in Selma for decades. Student Nonviolent Coordinating Committee members were on the scene, aiding the local activists in their work. In January 1965 Dr. King and the SCLC arrived in Selma to join the fight.

Opposite: Black voters cast their ballots in Alabama following the passage of the 1965 Voting Rights Act.

Alabama state troopers confront civil rights marchers at the Edmund Pettus Bridge in Selma, Alabama, on March 7, 1965. Leading the demonstrators are civil rights leaders John Lewis *(in light-colored overcoat)* and Hosea Williams.

BLOODY SUNDAY

The Selma campaign began with a series of demonstrations at the Dallas County courthouse. The courthouse held the local voter registration office and the headquarters of Sheriff Jim Clark. Clark was a fierce segregationist with a nasty temper. He and his deputies arrested thousands of demonstrators, including Dr. King. They also shoved, punched, and clubbed many of the peaceful protesters.

On February 18 the black residents of nearby Marion, Alabama, staged a sympathy march. A mob of lawmen and angry white citizens attacked. One of the marchers, black army veteran Jimmie Lee Jackson, was shot in the stomach by state troopers.

To protest Jackson's slaying, black activists organized another mass march. On Sunday, March 7, about six hundred demonstrators set out from Selma for the state capital, Montgomery. They planned to walk the entire fifty-four-mile route. They only made it a few blocks.

As the solemn procession crossed the Edmund Pettus Bridge, they were met by line after line of state troopers, sent by Alabama

THE CIVIL RIGHTS MOVEMENT

governor George Wallace to stop the march. The troopers ordered the marchers to turn around. Instead they got on their knees to pray. At that moment, recalled SNCC leader John Lewis, "all hell broke loose." The troopers charged into the crowd, swinging clubs and bullwhips. Then they opened fire with tear gas. Jammed on the bridge, the choking marchers scrambled to escape. Those who fled the scene were chased down and beaten. Miraculously no one was killed, but many people ended up in the hospital with serious injuries.

That evening ABC aired a special news bulletin. Viewers were stunned by the images of law officers savagely attacking unarmed men, women, and children on what quickly became known as Bloody Sunday. "It looked like war," recalled Selma mayor Joseph Smitherman. "That went all over the country. And the people, the wrath of the nation, came down on us."

When the marchers refused to back down, the troopers charged. John Lewis was hit twice on the head, and suffered a fractured skull.

A FUNERAL FOR JIM CROW

The day after Bloody Sunday, protest marches took place in dozens of northern cities. Supporters from as far away as New

Martin Luther King *(front row, second from right)* and his wife, Coretta, take the lead on the first day of the successful Selma-to-Montgomery march, March 21, 1965.

Thousands of people from all walks of life took part in the five-day march.

York and Minnesota began to arrive in Selma. On March 9 Martin Luther King led two thousand protesters to the spot on the Pettus Bridge where the troopers had attacked. The crowd knelt and prayed. Then they turned around and headed back to Selma. Dr. King had agreed not to violate a federal court order forbidding the march.

Many of the marchers felt let down by King's decision. The feelings of anger and betrayal reached a peak that night when James Reeb, a minister from Boston, was assaulted by white thugs in Selma. Reeb died two days later.

The third attempted Selma-to-Montgomery march began on March 21. The federal court had lifted its ban, and President Johnson had sent federal troops to guard the marchers. More than 3,000 people crossed the Pettus Bridge. They walked ten miles a day, singing their freedom songs. By the time they arrived in the capital, their numbers had swelled to nearly 25,000. Dr. King looked out over the sea of humanity. "I stand before you this afternoon," he said, "with the conviction that segregation is on its deathbed in Alabama and the only thing uncertain about it is how costly the segregationists

THE CIVIL RIGHTS MOVEMENT

and Wallace will make the funeral."

It was a triumphant moment. That night the joyous feelings were muted when segregationists claimed another victim. Viola Liuzzo, a white civil rights volunteer from Detroit, had been shot and killed by Ku Klux Klansmen.

Five months later, President Johnson signed the Voting Rights Act of 1965. The new law was the beginning of the end for Jim Crow. It banned literacy tests and other discriminatory voting requirements. It also gave the federal government the authority to oversee voter registration and elections. In the coming months, millions of southern blacks would proudly cast their first ballots, voting racist sheriffs, mayors, and other government officials out of office.

This young marcher smeared his face with sunscreen and wrote out his goal on his forehead.

"Burn, Baby, Burn!"

In August 1965 racial tensions exploded in the Watts section of Los Angeles, California. A white police officer had pulled over a black driver for drunk driving. As the two argued, a crowd began to gather. More policemen arrived. Suddenly, rocks and bottles were flying. The fighting quickly spread throughout the forty-five-square-mile neighborhood. Black rioters assaulted white drivers and set fire to white-owned businesses, shouting "Burn, baby, burn!" By the time the National Guard put down the riot six days later, thirty-four people were dead, more than a thousand had been injured, and millions of dollars in property had been destroyed.

Black leaders had been warning for years that violence was lurking just beneath the surface in America's cities. The successes of the civil rights movement in the South had done little to change daily life in black communities in other parts of the

country. Racial discrimination still restricted most blacks to overcrowded city ghettos. Persistent poverty, high unemployment, and police brutality contributed to the sense of anger and frustration. In the late 1960s the smoldering tensions would lead to riots in dozens of cities, including Newark, New Jersey; Detroit, Michigan; Cleveland, Ohio; and Chicago, Illinois.

After the passage of the Voting Rights Act, Martin Luther King decided that it was time to tackle the problem of discrimination in areas outside the South. King and the SCLC joined forces with local civil rights organizations to form the Chicago Freedom Movement. For nearly a year, black Chicagoans marched in white neighborhoods to protest housing segregation. Finally, protest leaders and city officials reached agreement on a program to promote equal housing opportunity. Declaring victory, Dr. King called off the marches. However, Chicago officials failed to keep their promises. Many African Americans who had participated in the protests denounced the agreement as a sellout. Their bitterness was just one more sign of the growing divisions in the civil rights movement.

BLACK POWER!

Many young black activists had begun to question the strategy of nonviolent protest. They had been discouraged by the failure of the Chicago Freedom Movement and other civil rights campaigns. At the same time, they had found inspiration in the speeches and writings of black nationalists, especially Malcolm X. To impatient young blacks, Martin Luther King and other older civil rights leaders seemed old-fashioned and out of touch. The young militants believed that it was time to stop *asking* for their rights and start *taking* them.

MALCOLM X

When Malcolm Little was an infant, his family was driven out of Omaha, Nebraska, by the Ku Klux Klan. When he was four, his father was killed by white supremacists in Lansing, Michigan. Malcolm spent the rest of his childhood in foster homes and a detention home for "juvenile delinquents." As a young man, he was arrested for burglary. While in prison, he discovered the empowering message of the Nation of Islam, also known as the Black Muslims.* This religious, political, and social movement led by Elijah Muhammad encouraged black nationalism. The black nationalists rejected the goal of integration. Instead, they called on African Americans to work together to build self-pride and economic and political independence.

After his release from prison, Malcolm became a minister for the Nation of Islam. Changing his name to Malcolm X, he traveled the country, urging African Americans to unite and take up arms in the "black revolution." He also encouraged black Americans to embrace their

Civil rights leader and Black Muslim minister Malcolm X

African heritage. "You can't hate the roots of the tree and not hate the tree," he said. "You can't hate your origin and not end up hating yourself; you can't hate Africa and not hate yourself."

In 1964 Malcolm X broke with the Nation of Islam. A year later, he was assassinated, mostly likely by Black Muslim rivals. His message of black pride and self-confidence lived on, however, inspiring African Americans to this day.

*For more on the Nation of Islam, see volume 8 in this series, *Marching toward Freedom.*

The first significant split in the civil rights movement came in 1965, after the Selma-to-Montgomery march. Student Nonviolent Coordinating Committee workers who had taken part in the march decided to remain in Alabama. They established a base in Lowndes County, a rural area with 12,000 black residents and only one black voter. SNCC began a project to register black voters and enroll them in a new political party, the Lowndes County Freedom Organization. In many ways their work was similar to the voter registration drives conducted during the 1964 Mississippi Freedom Summer. There were two significant differences, however. "The project staff took the strong position," said SNCC leader Stokely Carmichael, "[not] to allow whites [to participate]. . . . And we armed ourselves."

The symbol of the Lowndes County Freedom Organization was a snarling black panther. Other black nationalist organizations adopted the same symbol, along with the name Black Panthers. The largest and best known of these militant groups was the Black Panther Party for Self-Defense, founded in Oakland, California, by Bobby Seale and Huey Newton.

The Black Panther Party's demands for African Americans included justice, freedom, full employment, decent housing and education, and "an immediate end to police brutality and murder of black people." Party members wearing black leather jackets and berets patrolled the streets of Oakland, armed with shotguns. In May 1967 gun-carrying Black Panthers entered the California state legislature to protest a gun control bill. That act made the group a national sensation. Soon local chapters of the Black Panther Party were operating in cities all across the country. These groups not only guarded black communities from racism and police brutality but also developed

Black Panther Party founders Bobby Seale *(left)* and Huey Newton. Newton is wearing the group's trademark black beret and black leather jacket.

social programs such as free medical clinics and breakfast programs that fed thousands of needy schoolchildren.

Along with the Black Panthers, many other militant black organizations emerged during the late 1960s. Each of these groups had its own ideas, methods, and goals. Despite their differences, they all embraced the same battle cry: "Black Power."

"THE PROMISED LAND"

While moderate and radical black leaders often disagreed on goals and tactics, there was at least one area in which they were united: opposition to American involvement in the Vietnam War. African Americans opposed the war because it drained money and attention from domestic programs to combat poverty. They also argued that young black men were doing more than their fair share of the fighting and dying. Stokely Carmichael called U.S. involvement in Vietnam a case of "white people sending black people to make war on yellow people in order to defend the land they stole from red people."

In 1967 boxing champion Muhammad Ali, who had joined the Nation of Islam, refused to serve in Vietnam. Ali explained that "to bear arms or kill is against my religion." He also argued that a white draft board official who was a "descendant of the slave masters" had no right to order "a descendant of slaves to fight other people in their own country." Convicted of draft evasion, Ali was stripped of his world heavyweight title and banned from boxing for four years. He became a popular antiwar speaker both in the United States and abroad.

Martin Luther King also added his voice to the antiwar movement. In a speech in New York City in April 1967, he denounced the Johnson administration for "taking the black young men who had been crippled by our society and sending them eight thousand miles away to guarantee liberties in Southeast Asia which they have not found in southwest Georgia and East Harlem."

One year later, Dr. King traveled to Memphis, Tennessee, to support striking black sanitation workers. Speaking at a Memphis church on April 3, 1968, he looked back on the accomplishments of the civil rights movement. He called on blacks to reunite in their struggle "to make America what it ought to be . . . to make America a better nation." Concluding on a personal note, he proclaimed,

> We've got some difficult days ahead. But it doesn't matter with me now. Because I've been to the mountaintop. . . . And I've seen the promised land. I may not get there with you. But I want you to know tonight, that we, as a people, will get to the promised land.

The following day Martin Luther King Jr. was assassinated. Americans across the nation reacted with shock and sorrow to the loss of the great leader who had preached peace and understanding among the races. Thirteen-year-old Vincent Patton of Detroit "just couldn't believe that it had happened. . . . Who would do something like this?" William Rutherford, a member of Dr. King's staff, remembers seeing people in Atlanta "screaming and fainting and . . . tearing their clothing. It was just unbelievable." The grief and fury of black Americans soon erupted in riots in more than one hundred cities. The violence would rage for nearly three weeks, leaving forty-six people dead and more than two thousand injured.

Coretta Scott King attends funeral services for her slain husband at Ebenezer Baptist Church in Atlanta, April 9, 1968.

Dr. King's death completed the unraveling of the modern civil rights movement. His vision of a colorblind society had not been realized. But great barriers had been toppled, and tremendous progress had been made. As moderate and militant blacks went their separate ways, they would take the struggle to many different fronts. The dream of the "America that ought to be" would live on.

Glossary

accommodation The act of compromising with, or adapting to, an opposing point of view. *Accommodationism* often refers to the policy in which blacks adapt to the attitudes and expectations of whites.

civil rights The rights of U.S. citizens, especially the rights to personal liberty guaranteed by the 13th and 14th amendments to the Constitution and some acts of Congress.

emancipation Freeing someone from the control or power of another.

Jim Crow Laws and practices designed to segregate African Americans, stripping them of their political and civil rights; the Jim Crow system got its name from a ragged, clownish black character portrayed in nineteenth-century minstrel shows.

lynching A crime in which a lawless mob executes a person suspected of an offense.

Reconstruction The period from 1865 to 1877, during which the former Confederate states were placed under military rule before being readmitted to the Union.

segregation The practice of separating one race from another by setting up separate housing, schools, and other public facilities.

transatlantic slave trade The capture of men, women, and children in Africa and the transporting of those captives into slavery in the Americas.

To Find Out More

BOOKS

Altman, Linda Jacobs. *The American Civil Rights Movement: The African-American Struggle for Equality.* Berkeley Heights, NJ: Enslow Publishers, 2004.

Bohannon, Lisa Frederiksen. *Freedom Cannot Rest: Ella Baker and the Civil Rights Movement.* Greensboro, NC: Morgan Reynolds, 2005.

Finlayson, Reggie. *We Shall Overcome: The History of the American Civil Rights Movement.* Minneapolis, MN: Lerner Publications, 2003.

George, Charles. *Civil Rights: The Struggle for Black Equality.* San Diego, CA: Lucent Books, 2001.

Meltzer, Milton. *There Comes a Time: The Struggle for Civil Rights.* New York: Random House, 2001.

Treanor, Nick, ed. *The Civil Rights Movement.* San Diego, CA: Greenhaven Press, 2003.

Turck, Mary. *The Civil Rights Movement for Kids: A History with 21 Activities.* Chicago, IL: Chicago Review Press, 2000.

Wilson, Camilla. *Rosa Parks: From the Back of the Bus to the Front of a Movement*. New York: Scholastic, 2001.

Woog, Adam. *The Fight Renewed: The Civil Rights Movement*. Detroit, MI: Lucent Books, 2006.

Web Sites

African-American Odyssey: The Civil Rights Era. Library of Congress.
http://memory.loc.gov/ammem/aaohtml/exhibit/aopart9.html

Civil Rights in Mississippi Digital Archive: Oral History Index. University of Southern Mississippi.
http://www.lib.usm.edu/~spcol/crda/oh/index.html

National Civil Rights Museum.
http://www.civilrightsmuseum.org/gallery/gallery1.asp

Oh Freedom Over Me. American RadioWorks and American Public Media.
http://americanradioworks.publicradio.org/features/oh_freedom

Remembering Jim Crow. American RadioWorks and the Center of Documentary Studies, Duke University.
http://americanradioworks.publicradio.org/features/remembering

USA History: Civil Rights 1860–1980. Spartacus Educational.
http://www.spartacus.schoolnet.co.uk/USAcivilrights.htm

Selected Bibliography

Boyd, Herb. *We Shall Overcome*. Naperville, IL: Sourcebooks, 2004.

Carson, Clayborne, David J. Garrow, Gerald Gill, Vincent Harding, and Darlene Clark Hine, eds. *The Eyes on the Prize Civil Rights Reader*. New York: Penguin, 1991.

Fairclough, Adam. *Better Day Coming: Blacks and Equality, 1890–2000*. New York: Viking, 2001.

Franklin, John Hope, and Alfred A. Moss Jr. *From Slavery to Freedom: A History of African Americans*. New York: Alfred A. Knopf, 2000.

Gates, Henry Louis Jr., and Cornel West. *The African American Century: How Black Americans Have Shaped Our Country*. New York: Free Press, 2000.

Hampton, Henry, and Steve Fayer. *Voices of Freedom: An Oral History of the Civil Rights Movement from the 1950s through the 1980s*. New York: Bantam, 1990.

King, Martin Luther Jr. *I Have a Dream: Writings and Speeches That Changed the World*. Edited by James Melvin Washington. San Francisco, CA: HarperSanFrancisco, 1993.

Lewis, John, with Michael D'Orso. *Walking with the Wind: A Memoir of the Movement*. New York: Simon and Schuster, 1998.

Parks, Rosa, with Jim Haskins. *My Story*. New York: Dial Books, 1992.

Rubel, David. *The Coming Free: The Struggle for African-American Equality*. New York: DK Publishing, 2005.

Shapiro, Herbert. *White Violence and Black Response: From Reconstruction to Montgomery*. Amherst, MA: University of Massachusetts Press, 1988.

Williams, Juan. *My Soul Looks Back in Wonder: Voices of the Civil Rights Experience*. New York: Sterling, 2004.

Winters, Paul A., ed. *The Civil Rights Movement*. San Diego, CA: Greenhaven Press, 2000.

Notes on Quotes

Introduction
p. 8, "every single right": W. E. B. Du Bois, *The Autobiography of W. E. B. Du Bois* (New York: International Publishers, 1968), p. 250.

Chapter 1: The Montgomery Bus Boycott
p. 11, "Are you going to": Meltzer, *There Comes a Time*, p. 88.

p. 12, "I work hard all": Hampton and Fayer, *Voices of Freedom*, p. 25.

p. 13, "I was not tired" and "No, the only tired": Parks, *My Story*, p. 116.

p. 14–15, "My friends, there comes": Martin Luther King Jr. speech at Holt Street Baptist Church, December 5, 1955, at http://www.stanford.edu/group/King/papers/vol3/551205.004-MIA_Mass_Meeting_at_Holt_Street_Baptist_Church.htm

p. 16, "We shall match your": Alex Ayres, ed., *The Wisdom of Martin Luther King, Jr.* (New York: Meridien, 1993), p. 165.

p. 17, "chanted and sang": Fairclough, *Better Day Coming*, p. 233.

p. 19, "We had won self-respect": Hampton and Fayer, *Voices of Freedom*, pp. 32–33.

p. 20, "how to handle": Rubel, *The Coming Free*, p. 68.

p. 21, "galvanized the country": ibid., p. 74.

Chapter 2: The Little Rock Nine
p. 24, "destroy the system" and "resist forced integration": Boyd, *We Shall Overcome*, pp. 56–57.

p. 24, "with all deliberate speed": Carson and others, *The Eyes on the Prize Civil Rights Reader*, p. 96.

p. 26, "to protect the lives": Rubel, *The Coming Free*, p. 102.

p. 26–27, "From the time I": Hampton and Fayer, *Voices of Freedom*, p. 39.

p. 27, "Lynch her! Lynch her!": Carson and others, *The Eyes on the Prize Civil Rights Reader*, p. 102.

p. 27–28, "I don't think I": ibid., p. 103.

p. 29, "I'd only been": Hampton and Fayer, *Voices of Freedom*, pp. 45–46.

p. 30, "Nigger, nigger, nigger" and "had just picked up": ibid., pp. 49–50.

p. 31, "once I got as far": ibid., pp. 51-52.

Chapter 3: Sit-ins and Freedom Rides

p. 33, "We don't serve coloreds": Boyd, *We Shall Overcome*, p. 77.

p. 33, "mean and red": Carson and others, *The Eyes on the Prize Civil Rights Reader*, p. 115.

p. 34, "If it's possible": ibid.

p. 35, "moral obligation": Rubel, *The Coming Free*, p. 131.

p. 35, "We would do things": Hampton and Fayer, *Voices of Freedom*, p. 55.

p. 36, "Go home, nigger": Lewis, *Walking with the Wind*, p. 106.

p. 36, "hit in the ribs" and "mustard was squeezed": ibid., p. 107.

p. 38, "older folks": ibid., p. 114.

p. 38, "something much bigger": Carson and others, *The Eyes on the Prize Civil Rights Reader*, p. 120.

p. 39, "toughs grabbed the passengers": Lewis, *Walking with the Wind*, p. 146.

p. 40, "would effectively end": ibid., p. 148.

p. 41, "work was just beginning": ibid., p. 174.

Chapter 4: The Battle in Birmingham

p. 44, "a change in the attitude": Hampton and Fayer, *Voices of Freedom*, p. 113.

p. 44, "worst big city": Boyd, *We Shall Overcome*, p. 128.

p. 45, "a force and power": Boyd, *We Shall Overcome*, p. 111.

p. 45, "After the song": ibid., p. 115.

p. 45, "We shall overcome": Fairclough, *Better Day Coming*, p. 268.

p. 47, "legitimate and unavoidable impatience": King, *I Have a Dream*, p. 89.

p. 47, "I guess it is": ibid., p. 88.

p. 49, "shameful scenes": Fairclough, *Better Day Coming*, p. 278.

p. 49, "The Birmingham agreement": Rubel, *The Coming Free*, p. 199.

p. 49, "feverish, fragmented, almost uncontrollable": Fairclough, *Better Day Coming*, p. 274.

p. 51, "I say to you": King, *I Have a Dream*, p. 104.

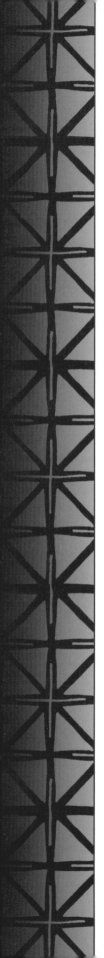

Chapter 5: Mississippi Freedom Summer

p. 54, "frail, bespectacled, and soft-spoken": Rubel, *The Coming Free*, p. 164.

p. 56, "would make it abundantly": Fairclough, *Better Day Coming*, p. 283.

p. 57, "It seemed to us": Boyd, *We Shall Overcome*, p. 172.

p. 57, "How can we put": ibid.

p. 57, "Maybe you won't laugh": Rubel, *The Coming Free*, p. 229.

p. 57, "I think it was": Boyd, *We Shall Overcome*, p. 172.

p. 58, "the young people": Hampton and Fayer, *Voices of Freedom*, p. 194.

p. 59, "back of the bus": Fairclough, *Better Day Coming*, p. 287.

p. 60, "that our task was": Rubel, *The Coming Free*, p. 241.

p. 60, "Freedom Summer was the": Hampton and Fayer, *Voices of Freedom*, p. 193.

p. 61, "I guess if I'd": Carson and others, *The Eyes on the Prize Civil Rights Reader*, p. 177.

p. 61, "We're not going to": ibid.

Chapter 6: To the Mountaintop

p. 65, "all hell broke loose": Lewis, *Walking with the Wind*, p. 327.

p. 65, "It looked like war": Rubel, *The Coming Free*, p. 254.

p. 66, "I stand before you": King, *I Have a Dream*, p. 122.

p. 67, "Burn, baby, burn!": Rubel, *The Coming Free*, p. 269.

p. 69, "black revolution": Carson and others, *The Eyes on the Prize Civil Rights Reader*, p. 258.

p. 69, "You can't hate": Cone, James M., *Malcolm X: The Impact of a Cultural Revolutionary* (*Christian Century*, December 23–30, 1992), at http://www.religion-online.org/showarticle.asp?title=167

p. 70, "The project staff took": Rubel, *The Coming Free*, pp. 268–269.

p. 70, "an immediate end": Boyd, *We Shall Overcome*, p. 223.

p. 70–71, "white people sending black people": Marqusee, Mike, *Redemption Song: Muhammad Ali and the Spirit of the Sixties* (London: Verso, 1999), p. 218.

p. 72, "to bear arms": Carson and others, *The Eyes on the Prize Civil Rights Reader*, p. 450.

p. 72, "descendant of the slave masters": ibid., p. 453.

p. 72, "taking the black young": King, *I Have a Dream*, p. 138.

p. 72, "to make America": ibid., p. 201.

p. 72, "We've got some difficult": ibid., p. 203.

p. 73, "just couldn't believe": "Where Were You the Day Martin Luther King Died?" American Forces Press Service, at http://www.defenselink.mil/news/newsarticle.aspx?id=43844

p. 73, "screaming and fainting": Hampton and Fayer, *Voices of Freedom*, p. 468.

Index

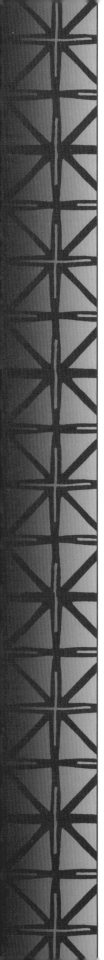